What does *become* mean and involve?
The third question is personal. *Can I personal Christian?* Can *I* be included in all this?

If so, the final question is practical—*How can to me?*

Christians claim that where you spend eternity depends on whether or not you are a Christian. The sands of time run out very quickly. If Christians are right you need to address this matter urgently.

The Lord Jesus Christ said, *If anyone thirsts let him come to Me and drink.* He promises to meet your thirst for forgiveness and reality if you believe in Him. But *how* can you *come* to Him? *How* do you *believe in* Him?

How can I become a Christian? is the most important question you can ever ask.

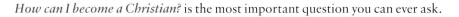

How can I become a Christian?

For some it is out of bounds to even consider *What is a Christian*? But to avoid misunderstanding, this question must be faced. First, what *cannot* make you become a real Christian? Second, how does the *Bible* describe a *Christian*?

You are not a Christian just because

you do things that Christians do, such as reading the Bible and Christian books, praying, keeping Sunday special as the Lord's day, or attending church services or Christian meetings. These may help your understanding, but no-one becomes a Christian just by doing them; **OR** you've gone through a ceremony of a church, such as baptism or confirmation. Millions of hypocrites, atheists, agnostics and merely nominally religious people have done that and are obviously not Christians. No religious ceremony—Christian or otherwise—can make you right with God; **OR** you belong to a

Christian family or church. Others' Christianity cannot be transferred to you. Becoming a Christian is personal; OR you sincerely live like a Christian and do good to others. Even a sincere, good living, generous, and helpful person can be as sincerely wrong as a blind man who walks unknowingly towards danger. Doing good cannot erase wrongdoing. God is offended by your many sins. You are lost and helpless without His forgiveness; OR you try not to lie, be selfish, get drunk, think or live immorally, act dishonestly, or harm others physically or mentally. Some non-Christians live like that too, so how can it make you into a Christian? ; OR you sincerely believe in God or admire Jesus Christ. So do many non-Christians; OR you live in a supposedly Christian country. There is no such thing as a truly Christian country and being a Christian does not depend on your geographical location;

5

OR you neither oppose Christian teaching, nor follow a different faith or belief, nor claim to be atheist, agnostic, or pagan. No-one becomes a Christian by not becoming something else! You cannot drift into faith in Christ by default. Becoming a Christian calls for God to work in your life as you trust in Christ.

How does the Bible describe a Christian?

The Bible uses the much-ridiculed word *saved* to describe a Christian. It also uses the phrase *child of God*.

JOHN 1:7

7 This man came for a witness, to bear witness of the Light, that all through him might believe.
8 He was not that Light, but was sent to bear witness of that Light.
9 That was the true Light which gives light to every man coming into the world.
10 He was in the world, and the world was made through Him, and the world did not know Him.
11 He came to His own, and His own did not receive Him.
12 But as many as received Him, to them He gave the right to become children of God, to those who believe in His name:
13 who were born, not of blood, nor of the will of the flesh, nor of the will of man, but of God.
14 And the Word became flesh and dwelt among us, and we beheld His glory, the glory as of the only begotten of the Father, full of

To be *saved* must imply that you are lost and need to be saved. The Bible says you are cut off from God by your sins and can do absolutely nothing to save yourself. Only when God saves you can you become a *child of God*.

A real Christian is a lost sinner who trusts only in the Lord Jesus Christ for forgiveness. Only Jesus can *save His people from their sins*. He **saves** a Christian in three ways.

First, Jesus HAS SAVED the Christian from sin's penalty. This deals with the PAST

God is holy and righteous. You have offended Him by your sins of thought, word, deed, motive and intent. You have sinned alone and with others, spontaneously and by design, deliberately and in ignorance. Sin is like a crime against God. God knows every sin you have committed and holds you culpable and accountable. He knows your "criminal record" of sins. Your guilt places you under God's sentence of eternal judgment.

CRIMINAL RECORD

Name Adam Smith
Date of birth: 1 January 1960
Conviction/Date
Theft: July 28 1995
Assault: Oct 15 1997
Fraud: Dec 3 2001

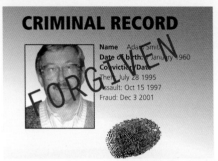

A Christian understands that in his, or her, place Jesus bore those sins and their punishment on the cross. If you are a Christian, Christ has saved you from sin's penalty. *FORGIVEN* is written across your guilty record. Jesus has paid for and cleared you of all your wrongdoing and guilt.

Second, Jesus is SAVING the Christian from sin's POWER. This applies NOW

As God convicts and awakens your conscience because of your sins against Him, He enables you to turn from them to Christ to be saved. Through the Holy Spirit, Christ enters and dwells in your heart to change you from within. God helps you every day as you have fellowship with Him by praying and reading His word, the Bible. He strengthens you to fight temptation and sin. He changes your attitude to sin. Although failing still, you no longer *plan* to sin. God continually prompts you to admit and turn from wrongdoing and seek His renewed forgiveness and cleansing. God's peace, joy and strength increase as Christ takes over the daily lordship of your life.

Third, Jesus WILL SAVE the Christian from sin's PRESENCE. This is for the FUTURE

You deserve eternal separation from God in Hell. But God guarantees that, because He has saved you, you will be in Heaven *with Christ* forever. After death, your soul will be *present with the Lord* and freed from sin's pollution. God promises also to give you a wonderfully changed resurrection body.

A child of God—in God's forgiven family

True Christian conversion occurs when, through the work of the Holy Spirit, a person becomes *born again*. That person has become a ***child of God***. The Christian receives from God a completely new inner and spiritual life. He or she is now one of God's family of forgiven, or *saved*, people.

Jesus told one religious leader that he could not enter the kingdom of God unless he became *born again*. He needed God's Spirit to enter him and radically change him into a *child of God*.

The Bible says of Jesus, that *as many as **received** Him, to them He gave the right to become **children of God**, to those who **believe in** His name: who were born, not of blood, nor of the will of the flesh, nor of the will of man, but of God.*

A drowning man needs to be rescued

To *receive* Christ means to *believe in His name*. You must trust completely in who Jesus is and in His death for you. The name *Jesus* means *God saves*. Jesus saves those who turn their backs on their sins and cast themselves wholly upon Him for mercy. He enters the life of every sinner who receives Him by believing in Him in that way. Imagine a drowning man. He is helpless and hopeless. He cannot save himself. Then his rescuer-to-be throws him a lifebelt. He can only be saved by clinging to that lifebelt. In the Biblical sense, he *believes in* that lifebelt. He can never boast about his swimming ability. Similarly, as a helpless and hopeless sinner, you can only *believe in* the Saviour when you know you cannot save yourself and cling to Him by faith. In gratefully receiving His mercy and forgiveness you *receive Him* into your life. As Christ enters your life through His Holy Spirit, you become *born again*, or *born of God*, and a member of God's family as a *child of God*.

11

Becoming a Christian is *not of blood* (you were not born a Christian), *nor of the will of the flesh* (you cannot do anything to save yourself from your sins), *nor of the will of man* (no-one else's plan, philosophy or religious requirements can save you.)

In summary, if you are a REAL Christian, this describes you

You are a guilty, lost and helpless sinner pardoned by God and indwelt by Him. Your sin is paid for and forgiven solely through Jesus' death on the cross for you. Having turned from your sins to Christ, He has entered your life through the Holy Spirit. God has made you His born again child. Your life is under His new management. God is changing you a little each day. You have been saved from eternal punishment in Hell. Heaven is now

your sure and certain home. You now want to live for God, despite your weaknesses, and you will seek to know and follow the Lord more closely as you go on with Him.

How can I become a Christian?

So a Christian is someone who is *saved* and has *become a child of God* by God's grace. You must *become a child of God* to know God's forgiveness. But some people say, "Surely, *everyone* is a child of God because He made us all." Are they right?

It is true that everything alive is a natural creature of God, from an eagle to an elephant, or from a fox to a fish, or from swine to swans. Humanity shares God as

Creator with eagles, elephants, foxes, fish, swine, swans and *all creatures great and small!* But such creatures can never become Christians! They are not in God's special family of saved, forgiven, born again children by faith in Christ. Neither animals nor human beings will ever become the forgiven and spiritual children of God simply by being alive.

To BECOME means being changed from what you were

You cannot *become* what you are already. To *become* a child of God implies that you must be changed.

A daffodil bulb must be changed to *become* a daffodil. A caterpillar must be changed to *become* a butterfly. Similarly, you need to be changed to *become* a child of God. The Bible says that only those who receive Christ *become* children of God. Only God can change you as you trust Christ.

If you have not become a child of God by receiving Christ, you are thus *not* a Christian.

You remain under God's sentence of wrath for your sins. You *urgently* need God to save you, by His grace, and thus make you *become* a child of God. Only then will you know God personally, be born again, have your sins forgiven, be changed by Christ indwelling your life and look forward confidently to Heaven.

You need to believe that Jesus died on the cross for you. You need to confess your sins with shame to God and turn from them by His strength. You need to receive Christ into your life by trusting Him. You need to be reconciled to God and *become* a real Christian.

How can I become a Christian?

Only God can make you into a Christian. No-one else can. People may pray and long that you become a Christian, but to become a child of God you must come to Christ, *personally*. An injured and dying victim of a road accident must have *personal* medical treatment at hospital to be saved. Similarly you must ask Christ *personally* and humbly to turn and save you from your sins.

I realised I was guilty and helpless

When I became a Christian, I realised that I had sinned against God and against other people. I was entirely to blame for my sins. I was guilty as charged and helpless to remove that guilt or conquer my sins.

I felt ashamed of all my selfish and wrong words, deeds, intents, motives, neglect, ignorance, hypocrisy and rebellion. Criticising others' shortcomings could not lessen my own guilt. If I pointed my finger at someone else, three fingers pointed at me, and my thumb pointed towards God, who knew everything about me.

The Judge could not be fooled—and no jury was needed

I knew from the Bible that I must appear before Christ as Judge. I had ignored God and rebelled against His righteous law. No jury was required to decide my guilt. God, the Judge, already knew the truth about me. He knew I was guilty and deserved His punishment.

Christ died for me

Jesus died on the cross as my substitute. Nailed there for me and crowned with thorns, He had borne my sins and suffered the eternal punishment that I deserved. He paid for my sins and then rose again from the grave.

The empty tomb

He conquered death, rose again, and is alive for evermore.

I prayed

In a silent prayer, I put my trust in Jesus Christ. I was so sorry for all my sins that I asked God to turn me from them. I urgently asked Jesus Christ to forgive and accept me, come into my life and control it.

The Bible came alive to me!

I read in the Bible of *the Son of God, who loved **me**, and gave himself for **me***. The double use of ***me*** assured me that this really was for ***me***.

Having received Christ, I could say—with every other real Christian – *I know whom I have believed*. I had come to know Jesus for myself. He would help me and keep me for Heaven.

It is no secret

A famous disk jockey became a Christian. The song he wrote as a result contains these words, *It is no secret what God can do.*
What He's done for others, He can do for you.
With arms wide open He'll pardon you.
It is no secret what God can do.

But *how can* God save you?

How can I become a Christian?

A question asked in different ways

A jailer in Philippi once asked *What must I do to be saved?* Some ask *How can I be forgiven?* or *How can I find God?* Others wonder *How can God accept me?* or *How can I be sure of going to Heaven when I die?* People often don't realize that the real question they are asking is, *How can I become a Christian?*

A question only answered in Jesus Christ

Jesus Christ, who *came into the world to save sinners*, was both fully God and entirely human, though sinless. He is the

> I am the way, the truth and the life. No one comes to the Father except through Me.

only **Person** who can save you from your sins. Consider His words, *I am the way, the truth, and the life. No one comes to the Father except through Me.* Remember that the name **Jesus** actually means *God saves*.

You can only be saved when you become His and He becomes yours. Jesus will hear and answer your cry from a repentant heart. Call on Him to save you, to enter your life, and to make you a child of God.

As a guilty, needy and lost sinner *you* are responsible to come to God for forgiveness. In mercy He will answer *you*, but *you* must cry to Him to save and help *you*, and control *your* life as your Lord. You must repent. Saving you is His work.

You must come to Him, not wait for Him to come to you.

Jesus told some: *you are not willing to come to Me that you may have life.* Some will be lost eternally because they refuse to repent and trust Christ.

He assures anyone coming to Him for forgiveness that *the one who comes to me I will by no means cast out*. He saves forever anyone coming to Him, however bad that person has been.

Are you burdened about your sins? Jesus welcomes you with these words: *Let not your heart be troubled; you believe in God, believe also in Me*. But beware! Just believing in God intellectually or superficially cannot save you: you must trust in Him with all your heart.

To those who really believe in Him the Bible says, *these are written that you may believe that Jesus is the Christ, the Son of God, and that believing you may have life in His name*. God's eternal life is a gift to possess now as well as a timeless reality.

If your trust in the risen Lord Jesus Christ is so real that you have a God-given desire to share your faith in Him with others, the Bible confirms that you are saved! The Bible says: *if you confess with your mouth the Lord Jesus and believe in your heart that God has raised Him from the dead, you will be saved. For with the heart one believes unto righteousness, and with the mouth confession is made unto salvation.* When you receive Christ in your life God counts you as righteous, despite your sins. As you confess to other people your faith in Jesus, God assures you of His pardon and acceptance and reinforces your growing faith in Him. *When your trust is in Jesus Christ you are built on Him as on a rock. Jesus Christ is far more solid, reliable and enduring than even the Rock of Gibraltar!*

Two crucified convicted criminals flanked Jesus as He died between them on the central cross. They blasphemously mocked Him. Then one of them realised that Jesus was entirely righteous, unlike him. He told the other criminal to stop mocking Jesus. He knew his own punishment was justly deserved. He then turned to Jesus and pleaded, simply and humbly: *Lord, remember me when You come into Your kingdom.*

That was his prayer. Just as the drowning man grasps the lifebelt thrown to him in his helplessness, this criminal grasped the pardon, forgiveness and eternal life only available in the Lord Jesus Christ.

He had no opportunity for Bible reading, churchgoing, baptism, holy communion, turning over a new leaf, charitable giving, or doing good works. He could neither help nor save himself. With shame, he honestly admitted his guilt. The sinless Saviour was dying for the sins that he, a convicted criminal, had committed. Jesus moved that convicted man to turn from his sins and trust Him, simply praying *Lord, remember me*.

That is how *you* must believe on Christ to receive Him into *your* life. Confess your own sins and turn away from them to Christ. See the righteous Son of God who died to pay for your sins. Pray humbly and personally to Him—*Lord, remember me!*

Assuredly, I say to you, today you will be with Me in Paradise

Jesus' reply to him was immediate, specific and personal: *Assuredly, I say to you, today you will be with Me in Paradise*. The man was promised a place immediately with Jesus.

Today Jesus Christ is in Heaven. Like that condemned man, cry to Him to save you. Believe in Him. Jesus has prepared a place in Heaven for those who believe in Him.

You need to pray, as that guilty, dying, convict did, *Lord, remember me!*

**How can I
become a**
real **Christian?**

Gerard Chrispin

Day One

*Check the Bible references
in this booklet*

This booklet reflects the teaching of the
Bible, God's word. The Bible verses
quoted below follow the order of the
headings in this booklet.

(As a guide, John 7:37-39 is John's
gospel chapter 7, verses 37 to 39.)

How can I become a real Christian?
John 7:37-39

How can I become a Christian?
Ephesians 2:8-9, Acts 16:31, John 1:12,
Romans 8:15-16,
1 John 3:1-2, Isaiah 59:2, Matthew
1:21, Romans 1:18, Hebrews 9:27, 1
Peter 2:24, 1 Peter 3:18,
John 3:36, Ephesians 3:17, Romans 8:9,
1 John 1:8-9, 2 Thessalonians 1:8-9,
John 14:2, 2 Corinthians 5:8,
Colossians 1:5, 1 Corinthians 15:51-54,
John 3:3 & 7, John 1:12-13, Jonah 2:9,
Romans 8:1, Romans 14:9, 2
Corinthians 5:7, Colossians 1:10.

How can I become a Christian? John
1:12, Ephesians 2:3, Romans 5:6 & 8, 1
Corinthians 15:3-4, 2 Corinthians 5:20.

How can I become a Christian? 1 Timothy 1:15, Hebrews 9:27, 1 Peter 4:5, Romans 1:18,
Isaiah 53:5-6, Matthew 28:6, Romans 8:34, Galatians 2:20, 2 Timothy 1:12.
How can I become a Christian? Acts 16:30, 1 Timothy 1:15, Acts 4:12, John 14:6, Romans 10:13, Matthew 11:28, Jonah 2:9, John 5:40, John 6:37, John 14:1, Deuteronomy 4:29, John 20:31, Romans 10:9-10, Luke 23:39-43, 1 Peter 1:3-4.

Read part of the Bible each day!
To know and follow Christ, you need to read the Bible. Why not start by reading thoughtfully some of John's gospel each day? Ask whoever gave you this booklet to help you obtain a Bible or a New Testament.

Further reading
Day One has other helpful booklets available. Two of these are *How can God accept me?* and *How can I find God?*.

Please write for a brochure for Day One's Christian books.

Other books by this author are:
The Resurrection—the unopened gift;
Philippians for today—Priorities from prison; Beyond Bars, and *The Bible Panorama— enjoying the whole Bible with a chapter by chapter guide!*

How can God accept me?

BY GERARD CHRISPIN
32 PAGES POCKET-SIZE
BOOKLET 50P
978 1 903087 09 1

Have you ever reflected on how bad you really are, and that you do need God's forgiveness and new life in Christ? Have you ever wondered if God really can put you right? This booklet pulls no punches, yet it carefully shows how you can come to know Christ, and experience God's complete pardon and acceptance. 32 pages of photo-illustrated text makes it easy to read and follow.

REFERENCE: EBK 1

How can I find God today?

GERARD CHRISPIN
32 PAGES POCKET-SIZE
BOOKLET 50P
978 1 84625 140 5

A photo-illustrated booklet showing that God is evident in His creation, that we are conscious of Him, that our consciences tell us we need Him, and that God speaks to us through the Bible and through Jesus Christ. Because Christ died on the cross for our sins, we will experience heart conversion if we come to Him as our Saviour and Lord.

REFERENCE: EBK 2

Please ask for details of discounts available for purchases of larger quantities